The Spiffy Screw

Julie Murray

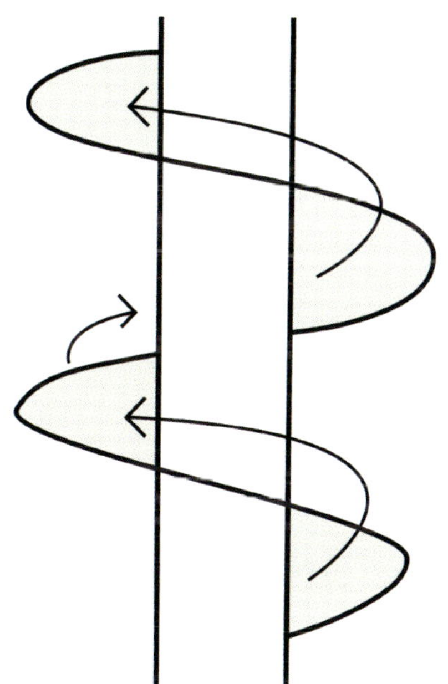

Abdo Kids Junior
is an Imprint of Abdo Kids
abdobooks.com

abdobooks.com

Published by Abdo Kids, a division of ABDO, P.O. Box 398166, Minneapolis, Minnesota 55439.

Printed in the United States of America, North Mankato, Minnesota.

052024

092024

Photo Credits: Getty Images, Shutterstock

Production Contributors: Teddy Borth, Jennie Forsberg, Grace Hansen

Design Contributors: Candice Keimig, Pakou Moua

Library of Congress Control Number: 2023948556

Publisher's Cataloging-in-Publication Data

Names: Murray, Julie, author.

Title: The spiffy screw / by Julie Murray

Description: Minneapolis, Minnesota : Abdo Kids, 2025 | Series: Simple machines | Includes online resources and index.

Identifiers: ISBN 9798384900627 (lib. bdg.) | ISBN 9798384901327 (ebook) | ISBN 9798384901679 (Read-to-me eBook)

Subjects: LCSH: Simple machines--Juvenile literature. | Screws--Juvenile literature. | Torque--Juvenile literature. | Machinery--Juvenile literature. | Hand tools--Juvenile literature.

Classification: DDC 621.8--dc23

Table of Contents

The Spiffy Screw

A screw is a simple machine.

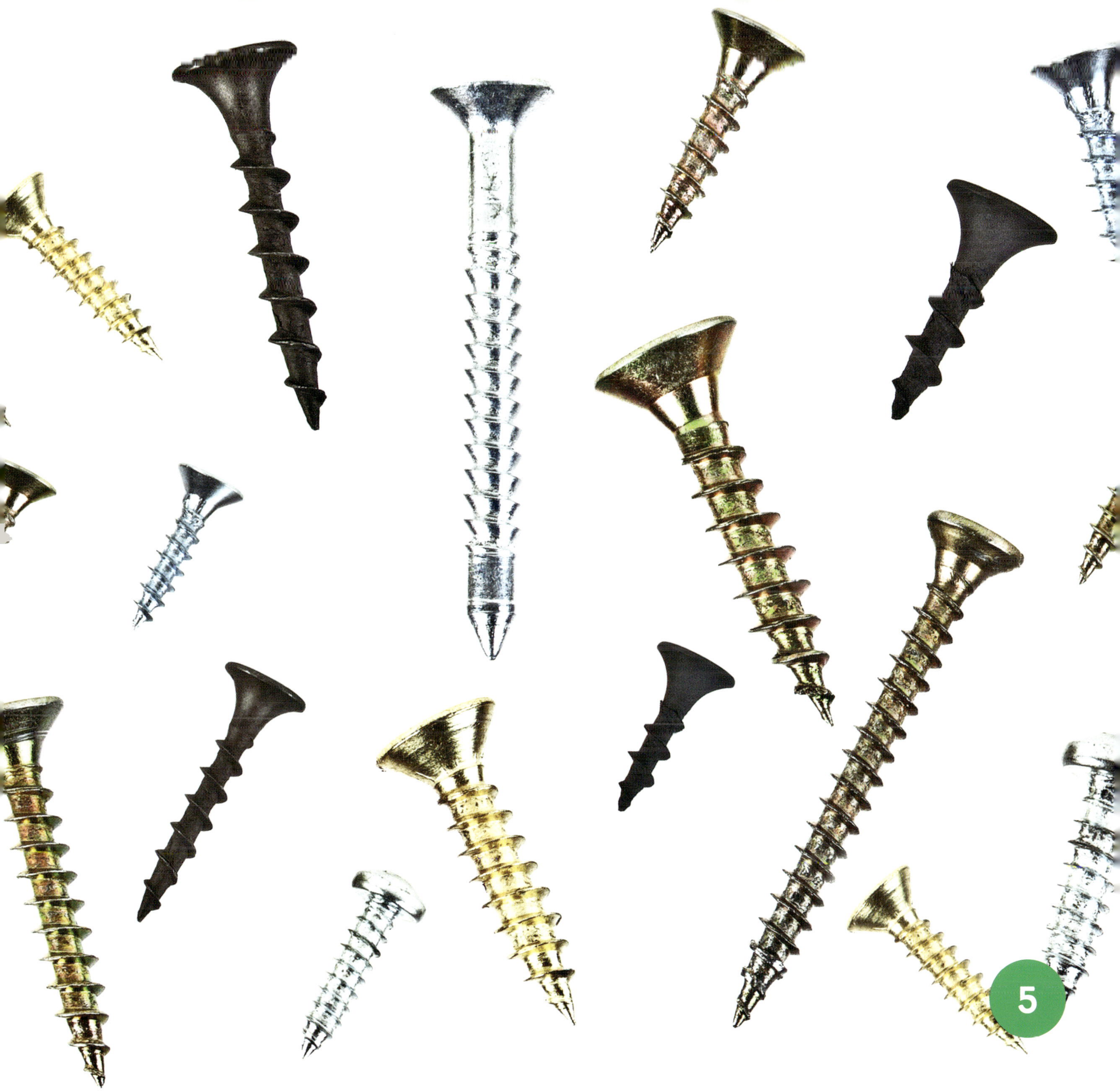

A screw can move an object higher or lower.

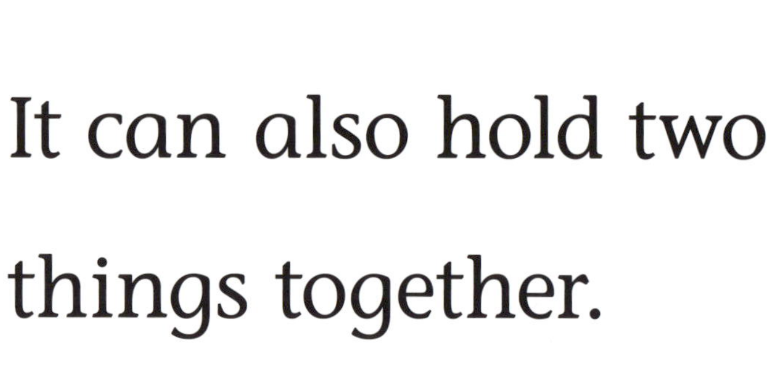

It can also hold two things together.

A screw is shaped like a **cylinder**.

A thread wraps around the **cylinder**. It is at an **angle**.

thread

Force is needed to use a screw.

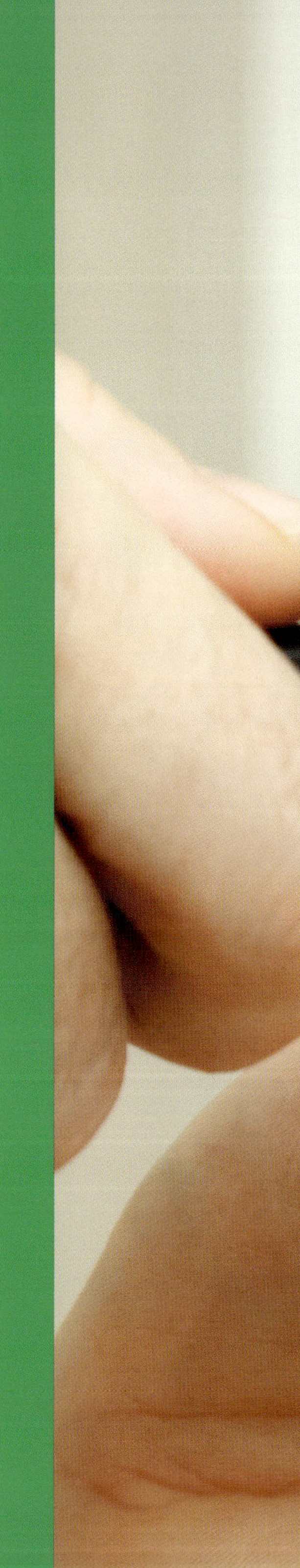

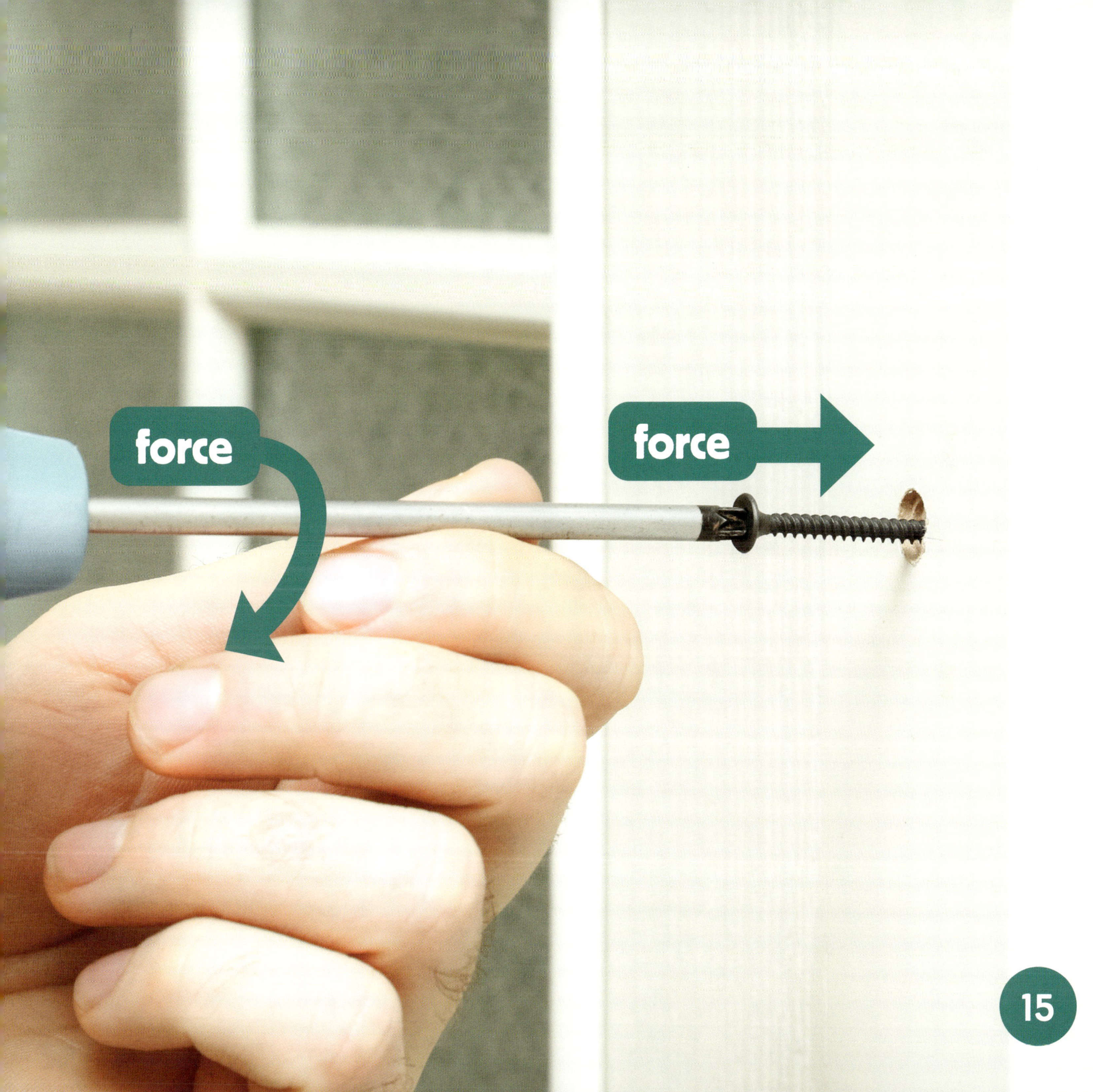
force
force

Force drives the thread up or down.

force

A jar lid is an example of a screw.

thread
thread

The screw makes work easier!

Screws Around You

auger

hose threads

light bulb cap

spiral staircase

Glossary

angle
a position that is not horizontal or vertical.

cylinder
a solid figure with a shape like that of a can.

force
power, energy, or physical strength.

Index

Visit **abdokids.com** to access crafts, games, videos, and more!

Use Abdo Kids code

STK0627

or scan this QR code!